J. B. Mattison

Treatment of Opium Addiction

J. B. Mattison

Treatment of Opium Addiction

ISBN/EAN: 9783337331160

Printed in Europe, USA, Canada, Australia, Japan

Cover: Foto ©Lupo / pixelio.de

More available books at **www.hansebooks.com**

THE TREATMENT

OF

OPIUM ADDICTION

BY

J. B. MATTISON, M.D.

Member of the American Association for the Cure of Inebriates; of the New York Neurological Society; of the Medical Society of the County of Kings, etc., etc.

NEW YORK & LONDON

G. P. PUTNAM'S SONS

The Knickerbocker Press

1885

TO

JOSEPH PARRISH, M.D.

OF

BURLINGTON, N. J.

WHO FIRST DIRECTED THE WRITER'S ATTENTION TOWARDS THE WORK TO WHICH HE
IS DEVOTING HIS PROFESSIONAL LIFE, THIS LITTLE BOOK—WITH THE
HIGHEST ESTEEM—IS MOST CORDIALLY INSCRIBED BY

THE AUTHOR

PREFACE.

———

This monograph is—mainly—a paper presented to the American Association for the
Cure of Inebriates at its last annual meeting,
October 22, 1884, and details a method of
treatment original with the writer, and practised
by him for several years with increasing satis-
faction and success.

BROOKLYN, N. Y.,
314 State St., *June* 1, 1885.

v

THE TREATMENT

OF

OPIUM ADDICTION.

SEVERAL years have passed since the writer had the pleasure of reading before this society a paper on the subject of opium addiction.

During this time his professional attention has been largely, and, of late years, exclusively devoted to the study and treatment of this toxic neurosis, and, with increasing experience has come improved therapeutics, all of which warrant him in again inviting attention to a topic that, though accorded but little thought by the profession at large, possesses a great and growing importance, the extent of which, perhaps, will be none the less appreciated by the reflection that many of those who fall victims to its steady advances are recruited from the ranks of our own confrères.

Opium addiction is a *disease*, a well-marked

functional neurosis, and deserving recognition as such to a greater degree than it has hitherto received. In the vast majority of cases the *vice* theory of its origin is incorrect, so that, with few exceptions, the term "opium habit" is a misnomer, implying, as it wrongly does, an opiate-using quite under individual control.

As elsewhere stated, " The Genesis of Opium Addiction," *Detroit Lancet*, Jan., 1884, two causative factors exist—necessity and desire,— but the result, if the opiate be sufficiently long continued, is essentially the same—a condition of disease, as evidenced by various functional ills.

The central tracts involved are the cerebro-spinal and sympathetic systems. Deviations from health noted are due to departure from the normal tone of one or both of these centres. Organic lesions are rare—possibly some instances of renal or brain disease,—the usual ultimate result being a state of marasmus—impaired nutrition, and profound nerve depression—ending in death.

In the paper to which reference has been made, attention was invited to a new method of treatment, and as this is largely the same we now employ—some improved changes will be noted in passing—we re-assert that it is based on the power of certain remedial resources to control abnormal reflex sensibility, and accomplishes, largely, two cardinal objects : minimum duration of treatment and maximum freedom from pain.

It is a fact well attested by clinical observation, that the ravages of opium-excess are spent mainly on the nervous systems before noted, inducing changes that give rise to great nervous disturbance when the opiate is peremptorily withdrawn—unless some mitigating measure be interposed,—and which, even in the process of very gradual withdrawal, is seldom, if ever, entirely avoided.

A recital of the varied symptoms of abrupt opiate-renouncing is not here needed. Let it suffice to say we regard them all, certainly the most important—the aches, pains, yawnings, sneezings, shiverings, nausea, vomiting, diarrhœa, restlessness, delirium, convulsions, exhaustion, collapse,—as reflex indications of great irritation in those centres, and any method having the power to counteract and control this condition must contribute vastly to the patient's comfort and cure.

Heretofore, two plans have obtained in the

treatment of opium addiction. One, which may well be called heroic, the entire and abrupt withdrawal of the usual opiate, invariably gives rise to great distress of mind and body, to relieve which various remedies are, at the time, resorted to. Those not fully informed, and desirous of knowing the extent of this suffering, which is far from imaginary, as some would have us believe, should consult Levinstein's work, in which are given details of twenty-four cases of hypodermic morphia addiction treated by this method, which the author, by a process of logic neither safe nor sound, declares to be the best. *This statement we emphatically dispute.* No treatment that entails such suffering as in the cases cited can claim pre-eminence over one more humane and equally effective. A study of the resultant effects in the instances alluded to reveals evidence of dire distress, in seven cases so extreme—perilous collapse— that a temporary return to hypodermic morphia became imperative to avert a fatal termination.

The other plan, consisting in a very gradual decrease of the usual opiate, meanwhile toning up the system to make amends for the accustomed narcotic, secures the desired result at much less discomfort, and we know of no reason why it should not be just as permanent. It is, however, open to the objection of requiring a much more protracted treatment—a point of importance when time is limited,—while it also tends to exhaust the patient's patience, and many refuse to continue till success is secured.

The method we commend is a mean between these extremes, and consists in producing a certain degree of nervous sedation and consequent control of reflex irritation by means of the bromides, though we refer, specifically, to the *bromide of sodium*, having used that exclusively in cases under our care. This plan, which, so far as we are aware, is original with ourselves, is merely a new application of a well-established principle, for the power of the bromides to subdue abnormal reflex irritability is so constant that it may be looked upon as an almost invariable sequel of such medication. Dr. Ed. H. Clarke, in his valuable treatise on the bromides, says : " Diminished reflex sensibility, however different physiologists may explain the fact, is one of the most frequent phenomena of bromidal medication that has been clinically observed, and is, therapeutically, one of the most important." The testimony of other observers is to the same effect, Gubler, Guttman, Laborde, Voison, Damourette, Eulenberg, Claude Bernard, Brown-Séquard, and Echeverria, all giving evidence as to the power of these agents over abnormal reflex action, and at the same time over the general nervous system. Admitting that the symptoms of opiate-disusing pertain almost exclusively to the domain over which the bromides exert so decided a control, we have a new field presented for the exercise of this valuable power, and the fact, proven conclusively by our experience, that it *does* exert this happy effect, fully supports the idea advanced as to the pathology of this disease.

In speaking of the bromide of sodium, let it be understood that we refer entirely to the influence of the *continued dose*, by which we mean its administration twice in the twenty-four hours, at regular intervals, so as to keep the blood constantly charged with the drug. A most important difference exists between the effect of this mode of exhibition and that of the single dose, or two or three doses so nearly together as to form practically one, for, in the former case, the system is constantly under the bromide influence, while in the other, the drug being largely eliminated in a few hours, the blood is nearly free from it a large portion of the time. Results obtainable from the continued use cannot be gotten from the single dose, and, as a consequence, its value is far greater in the disease under consideration.

Again, the action of the continued dose being somewhat remote—three to five days usually elapsing before there is decided evidence in this direction,—much more desirable results are secured by its employment for several days *prior* to an entire opium abandonment, meanwhile gradually reducing the opiate, than if the withdrawal be abrupt and then reliance placed on the bromide ; for, in the one instance, the maximum sedative effect is secured at the time of maximum nervous disturbance from the opium removal, and its counteracting and controlling influence is far in excess of that to be had from its employment after the lighting up of the nervous irritation. What, then, we term *preliminary sedation* forms a peculiar and valuable feature in our giving of the bromide, and it is this special point we commend, our experience having convinced us that we have in it an un-

equalled means of obviating the discomfort
incident to the treatment of this disorder.

The value of the various bromides depends
on their proportion of bromine. Bromide of
potassium contains 66 per cent., sodium 73,
and lithium 92 per cent. We should, therefore, expect a more powerful influence from
the last agent, and, according to Weir
Mitchell, it has a more rapid and intense effect.
The sodium, however, answers every purpose,
and has several points in its favor over the
other bromides : is pleasanter to the taste, more
acceptable to the stomach, causes little cuta-
neous irritation, and much less muscular prostration. In this connection, recent experi-
ments and observations by Drs. Ringer and
Sainsbury on the superior value of the sodium
salt are of interest, and may be found in the
British Medical Journal, Mar. 24, 1883.

Either of the bromides, in powder or con-
centrated solution, is somewhat irritant, sometimes producing emesis, and in any event, de-
laying its absorption. A practical point, then, is
that it be given largely diluted. Dr. Clarke
says : " There should be at least a drachm of
water to each grain of the salt." We give
each dose of the sodium in six or eight ounces

of cold water, and have never known it to cause vomiting.

To secure the requisite degree of sedation within a limited period, it is essential that the bromide be given in full doses. We are convinced that failure from its use, in any neurosis, is very often due to a non-observance of this point. Our initial dose of the sodium is 60 grains, twice daily, at twelve hours' intervals, increasing the amount 20 grains each day, *i. e.*, 70, 80, 90 grains, and continuing it five to seven days, reaching a maximum dose of 100 to 120 grains twice in twenty-four hours. During this time of bromidal medication, the usual opiate is gradually reduced, so that from the eighth to the tenth day it is entirely abandoned. A decrease of one quarter or one third the usual daily quantity is made at the outset, experience having shown that habitués are almost always using an amount in excess of their actual need, and this reduction occasions little or no discomfort. Subsequently, the opiate withdrawal is more or less rapid, according to the increasing sedation, the object being to meet and overcome the rising nervous disturbance by the growing effect of the sedative ; in other words, maximum sedation at the time of maximum irritation.

Exceptions to this may occur. Some patients are so weak and anæmic, on coming, that a previous tonic course is deemed judicious ; the usual opiate is continued for a time, and, meanwhile, with good food, tonics, and other measures, an effort is made to improve the impaired condition, and with success, for we have seen patients gain markedly in strength and weight during this roborant régime.

Sometimes a patient, before placing himself under our care, has reduced his daily taking to the lowest amount consistent with his comfort. If so, the initial large reduction is not made, but the decrease is gradual throughout. Again, in some instances no reduction is made for two or three days, at the end of which the bromide effect is secured in part, and the decrease is then begun. And in all instances this rule governs : *each case is a law unto itself, and the length and amount of the bromide-giving and consequent rate of opiate decrease is determined entirely by individual peculiarity as shown both before and during treatment.*

Surprise may be expressed and objection

made regarding the extent of the bromide doses, but the fact must never be overlooked that we are not to be governed in the giving of any remedy by mere drops or grains, but by the *effect produced*. Again, one effect of opium addiction is a peculiar non-susceptibility to the action of other nervines, necessitating their more robust giving to secure a decided result. More, under the influence of certain abnormal conditions, doses which, ordinarily, are toxic become simply therapeutic. The annals of medicine abound with instances in support of this statement, and among the most striking may be noted the following : Dr. Southey read before the Clinical Society of London notes of a case of tetanus which occurred in a boy ten years old. The first symptoms of trismus were observed two days after a severe fright and drenching due to the upsetting of a water butt. They steadily increased up to the date of his admission to St. Bartholomew's Hospital, on the eighth day of his illness, when the paroxysms of general opisthotonos seized him at intervals of nearly every three minutes. Each attack lasted from fifteen to thirty seconds, and although between the seizures the muscles of the trunk became less rigid, those of the neck and jaw were maintained in constant tonic cramp. The patient was treated at first with chloral, ten grains, and bromide of potassium twenty grains, every two hours, and afterward with the bromide alone in sixty-grain doses every hour and a half. When about two ounces were taken in twenty-four hours, the attacks became less frequent, but at first each separate seizure was rather more severe, and on the evening of the eleventh day he was able to open his mouth better. On the thirteenth day the bromide was decreased to twenty grains every three hours, and on the fourteenth day was discontinued altogether. When the bromide had been omitted twenty-four hours the attacks returned at intervals of an hour, and the permanent rigidity of the muscles of the neck was re-established. His condition now steadily became worse, so that on the eighteenth day of his illness it became necessary to resort to the previous large doses, one drachm every hour and a half. After three such doses the expression become more natural, and he was able to open his mouth again ; but it was not until the twenty-fifth day of the disease that it was possible to discontinue the remedy. The patient remained in a state of remarkable prostration and drowsiness, sleeping the twenty-four hours round, and only waking up to take his food for eight days, and passed all his evacuations under him. He subsequently steadily and rapidly convalesced. The bromide produced no acne or other disagreeable effect, and certainly seemed to exert a markedly controlling influence upon the tetanus.

Surely, under ordinary circumstances, no one would think of giving such doses of bromide ; but here, under the antagonizing influence of the intense reflex irritation, their effect was vastly beneficial, conducing, beyond question, to the patient's cure.

Given as we commend, no effect is usually noted before the second or third day. Then patients mark an increasing drowsiness, which deepens into slumber, more or less profound, so much so, at times, that it is difficult to remain long awake. With this is a growing aversion to active exercise, not solely due to lessened muscle force, but largely to mental hebetude. Some cases are met with in which the hypnotic effect is not very decided, but the rule is as stated. Sometimes a saline taste and increased saliva with the bromic breath are noted, and the tongue becomes furred. Acne is usually absent. The renal secretion is almost invariably largely augmented. We have known patients to pass more than one hundred ounces in the twenty-four hours, and we have noticed this, that where the renal activity is not increased, or is diminished, the sedative effect of the drug is more prompt and decided. The practical point of this is obvious : such cases require a less-prolonged bromide-giving.

With some there is slight transient loss of co-ordinating power in the fingers, and, exceptionally, in unusually sensitive subjects, there may occur mild startings of the forearm tendons. These, however, soon subside, and their going is largely hastened by local faradic séances.

Another bromide symptom, and a curious one it is, relates to a peculiar form of aphasia, as shown by using one word for another,— Brown for Jones, cake for comb, etc. This may persist for several days. Dr. Clarke refers to several such instances, and says : " They are hints of a distinct organ of language, and suggest the notion that, inasmuch as the drug we are considering paralyzes reflex before it does general sensibility, language may be the expression or correlation of a peculiar reflex power."

Another similar symptom is an odd effect on the memory, the loss of a word or a sentence, and entire inability to regain them at the time, so that the train of thought is abruptly ended. These, though often amusing, are sometimes quite annoying to the patient, but possess no other importance, and soon pass away.

Before dismissing this phase of the treatment we must again insist upon the fact that all cases of opium addiction do not require the bromide alike. This is a point of prime importance, and failure to put it in practice is, doubtless, often the main secret of ill success or unpleasant results in its use. The patient, as well as his disease, must be treated, and he who uses the bromide, as Fothergill asserts Opie mixed his colors—" with brains "—will accomplish far more than the tyro who sets himself up in the treatment of this or any other disorder, and fails to be guided by good judgment. To follow a mere routine-giving of the bromine, or any other remedy, unvaried by individual condition, is a sorry showing of professional incapacity. We have lately learned of a case of this kind, presenting a lamentable lack of discretion. The patient, a medical man, addicted to morphia, having decided upon self-treatment, began a plan of operations with the bromide, taking it himself for several days, and then its hypnotic effect asserting itself, he gave orders that it should be given him some days longer, and this senseless advice being blindly followed by his attendant, he sank into a stupor which persisted for more than a fortnight. A more indiscreet performance is seldom heard of, and illustrates anew, in another sense, the truth of that trite legal proverb as to the mental status of the individual who is both lawyer and client. Let it be distinctly understood that some cases of opium addiction are ineligible for the bromide treatment. Those complicated with serious lesion of heart or lungs should be excluded, and those in which there is marked general debility should always be accorded a previous tonic course. Lastly, as before asserted, *in each and every case where it is given, the extent of its continuance is to be governed entirely by individual peculiarities as indicated both before and during treatment.*

We now desire to call attention to another point, which our experience has convinced us

is of value. We refer to the treatment just
after the habitual hypodermic or other opiate
is abandoned. Supposing a case where, at the
end of five to seven days, as individual peculiarity may determine, the desired sedation is
secured and the usual opiate reduced to a
minimum—say $\frac{1}{6}$ to $\frac{1}{2}$ gr. each dose—in-
stead of an entire discontinuance, we change
the order of affairs and make a break in upon
the routine-taking—the "habit," so to speak—
by giving one full dose, by mouth, in the evening. This ensures a sound, all-night sleep,
from which the patient awakes greatly re-
freshed, and often quite surprised at his good
condition, which usually persists during the
day. The next evening at about the same
hour, the maximum bromide dose and two
thirds of the previous opiate are given ; the
third evening, the same amount of bromide and
one third the first evening's opiate. This ends
both opiate and bromide. Exceptionally, the
full single dose of opium and sodium is given
only one or two evenings. During the following day, if the patient be quiet, nothing is
given. Should there be minor discomfort, one-
half-ounce doses of fld. ext. coca, every second hour, have a good effect. Cases occasion-

ally require nothing else. If, however, as usually occurs, despite the coca, the characteristic restlessness sets in, we give full doses of fld. ext. cannabis indica, and repeat it every hour, second hour, or less often, as may be required. When the disquiet is not marked, this will control. If more decided measures be called for, we use hot baths, temp. 105° to 112°, of ten to twenty minutes' duration, and repeated as required. A short shower or douche of cold water often adds to their value. Nothing equals them for this purpose. Warm baths are worthless. The water must be *hot*—as much so as one can bear. We have repeatedly known a patient to fall asleep while in the bath.

And, just here as to "full doses" of the hemp. The dose of the books is useless. As before stated, addiction to opium begets a peculiar tolerance of other nervines, and they must be more robustly given. We give sixty minims Squibbs' fld. ext., repeated as mentioned, and have never noticed unpleasant results. Small doses are stimulant and exciting, large ones sedative and quieting; hence the latter are seldom followed by the peculiar haschish intoxication. And, lest some timid reader should regard this as reckless dosing, we hope to calm his fears by saying that the toxic power of hemp is feeble, and that these doses are the result of an experience of the drug in many cases in which smaller ones have failed of the desired effect.

At this writing, two lady convalescents, still insomniac, are nightly taking these full doses with good effect in securing sleep. One re cent lady patient, who did not lose a single night's slumber during treatment, and whose need for a soporific ended in eight days, took no other hypnotic whatever. We have used it of late more largely than ever, and with growing confidence in its sleep-giving power; taking, in this regard, almost exclusively, the place of chloral.

Regarding this insomnia, Levinstein and other German writers assert that it will " resist every treatment during the first three or four days." This may be true with them, considering their method, and is, of itself, added proof that they are lamentably lacking in the therapeutics of this disease. Under the plan we pursue no such sleepless state is noted, and in ordinary, uncomplicated cases, patients can usually be promised recovery without the loss of a single entire night's slumber.

Chloral, during the first four or five nights of opium abstinence, fails as a soporific, often causing a peculiar excitement or intoxication—patients talking, getting out of bed and wandering about the room—followed, it may be, after several hours, by partial sleep.   Later, in full doses—we prefer 45 grs. at once, rather than three 15-gr. doses,—alone, or with a bromide, it can be relied on as an hypnotic, but we have thought that, in some cases, where it secured sleep, patients, the next morning, felt a certain languor, of which it was largely the cause.   Some who use the hemp mention a feeling of fulness about the head and eyes, with occasional confusion of thought, but seldom complain of pain, having noted only one such case.

The bromide, baths, hemp, and coca, with or without capsicum—of which more later,—are, therefore, the main remedies for the restlessness and insomnia, two symptoms which, with a third, sneezing, are invariable sequelæ of opium withdrawal, and, wanting which, patient is surely deceiving his physician.

For relief of neuralgic pains in various parts, which sometimes occur, varied measures suffice. At the head of the list are electricity and the local application of ether. As to the value of the galvanic current in migraine and other neuralgiæ so common in opium habitués, and the manner of using it, the reader is referred to papers on "The Prevention of Opium Addiction," in the *Louisville Medical News*, Feb. 23, 1884, and *Boston Medical and Surgical Journal*, May 7, 1885. The same agent is effective in relieving limb and lumbar pains, though here a much stronger current is required than can be used with safety about the head. Sometimes a strong faradic current acts well, and where one fails, trial should always be made with the other. Local hot baths—sitz or foot —are often of great service for this purpose. Chloroform, locally, relieves ; so, too, massage.

Regarding the ether, those who have never employed it will, we are sure, be surprised at its pain-easing power. It matters not how it be applied—spray, drop, or lavement—it is potent for good.

These three—electricity, ether, hot water— are our main anodynes, and one special point in their favor is entire freedom from unpleasant gastric or other results.

For relief of minor neuralgic pains, other remedies, at times, suffice. Croton, chloral, in ten-gr. doses, every hour, is sometimes quite effective in tri-facial disorder. Tonga, one drachm of fluid extract, every hour, is often a reliable anodyne. Its value in some cases seems increased by combining it with the various salicylates. Caffeine or guarana occasionally relieves.

Externally, menthol, in solution, two drachms to the ounce of alcohol, used with a brush, as a spray, or the menthol cone, is sometimes of service. So, too, the well-known camphor and chloral combination, bi-sulphide of carbon, and various minor local anæsthetics.

Under this plan of treatment, marked disorder of stomach or bowels is rare. Our rule is to give an active mercurial or other cathartic, at the outset, if there be evidence of alvine disorder, and then secure regular action by such laxative as is found most agreeable. If the latter be so relaxed as to require restraint, thirty-minim doses fld. ext. coto, or sixty-gr. doses of subnit. bismuth, every two to four hours, often serve a good purpose. They are best given in capsule. If, however, the diarrhœa persists more than twenty-four hours, the most effective measure is to give a full opiate —tinct. opii., per mouth or rectum preferred—

at bedtime. This promptly controls, gives a full night's sleep, and the trouble seldom returns. Fear of an untoward effect on convalescence is unfounded. With our experience, the assertion of one writer that " it is impossible to cure the opium habit, and bridge the patient over the crisis, without having the bowels freely relaxed," seems quite absurd. We have again and again seen patients recover who had only two, three, or four movements daily. One such, lately dismissed, was a hypodermic taker of twenty grs. morphia, daily, and had been addicted for several years. Others have required a laxative enema in less than a week after the opiate withdrawal.

Formerly, an exclusive milk and lime-water diet during the first two or three days of opium abstinence was deemed advisable. This régime is not now imposed, as some patients are able to do dietetic duty, and the rule is to make no restriction unless the exceptionally occurring stomach or bowel trouble seems to require. More than one patient, habitués for years, did not vomit once. The excessive vomiting mentioned by Levinstein and Obersteiner—they practise abrupt disuse—we have never noted. The former thinks the collapse

—which we have never seen—observed in several of his cases was due to the vomiting and purging. Probably the largest factor in causing it was the exhausting general mental and physical suffering which his monstrous method entails.

If the stomach rebels, entire rest, abstinence from solid food, or all food, for a time, milk and lime water, or Murdoch's food, in small amount, often does well. If more active measures be required, sinapisms, ether, faradism externally, and, internally, bismuth, chloroform, menth. pip., ice, are of value. If all fail, a full opiate, hypodermic, will promptly suffice.

Having thus crossed the opiate Rubicon, treatment relates, largely, to the debility and insomnia. For the former, of internal tonic-stimulants, coca leads the list. But our experience does not warrant Morse's assertion —"coca cures the opium habit." That is a mistake. While it is of great value in relieving the varied symptoms of lessened nerve tone, it is *not a specific.* Patients, long used to opium, cannot abandon it and trust to coca alone, to carry them over the crisis. This, save in mild cases, it will not do, but, conjoined

with other measures, it is strong for good. Of
a reliable fluid extract, we give it sometimes
before, and always after, the acute restlessness,
in four- to eight-drachm doses, every two hours,
or less often as required, and continue in these
full doses, at increasing intervals for several
days. As need for it lessens we decrease the
dose to one or two drachms, and this amount,
ter die, combined with other tonics, may sometimes be continued with advantage for weeks.
As a rule, however, its use is quite abandoned
within a fortnight. Its effect, while noted in
from three to twenty minutes, seldom persists
more than two or three hours, so that, when
the demand for it is active, it is best given at
this interval. To remove the mental and
physical depression, the minor neuralgiæ, and
the occasionally occurring desire for stimulants
observed in these cases, nothing equals it, being in this regard more nearly a specific than
any drug at command ; and capsicum, in doses
of one half to one drachm of the tincture, with
the coca often adds to its value.

On the discovery of cocaine, it was thought
its use, hypodermically, might prove of value
in the treatment of this disorder, and, on asserted foreign authority, somewhat extrava-

gant statements were made of its merit in this regard ; but repeated trials by the writer have failed to prove them, and, in his opinion, it is much inferior to a reliable fluid extract of coca.

Another agent of much service is general faradization, twenty-min. séances daily, the feet on a plate to which the negative pole is attached, while the other electrode, encased in a large sponge well wet with warm water, is applied to the entire surface, with a current strong enough to be thoroughly felt, but not painful. This imparts a grateful sense of exhilarating comfort, and is the most effective tonic at command. Thus applied, or with anode to cervical spine, it may be used, daily, so long as indicated, taking care not to overdo, for a current too strong or prolonged works mischief, overstimulating and exhausting to the extent, it may be, of several days' discomfort, which nothing but time will remove. Very exceptionally, faradism disagrees and has to be abandoned.

Alternating with or following we may use the galvanic current. This is a general tonic of special value in these cases. Our method is, positive pole to nape of neck, and negative to epigastrium for five minutes; then the former behind the angle of each jaw for one or two minutes, making the entire séance of seven to nine minutes.

Next to the electric tonic ranks the cold shower bath. It certainly is a great invigorator, and many a patient who dreads it at first, soon comes to appreciate it most highly. If agreeing, it should always be taken. With some it acts as an hypnotic. We recall one instance, in particular, of a medical gentleman, who, still somewhat insomniac, after sleeping two or three hours and awaking with no prospect of further sleep, would take a shower, followed by vigorous rubbing, and soon fall into a refreshing slumber lasting till morning.

Internal tonics, of course, have a place in the roborant régime, varied as the case may demand. In some cases we employ them from the outset, and the use of tinct. ferr. mur. in large doses—fifteen to twenty min. thrice daily— has seemed, in virtue of its tonic-astringent effect, to serve a doubly good purpose in lessening the tendency to alvine relaxation. After the opiate disuse, an excellent combination is fld. ext. coca with syr. hypophosphites iron, strychnine, and quinine, two drachms of each after meals. Another, Fowler's solution or tinct. nux vomica with dilute phosphoric acid or acid phosphate. If anæmic, ferric tincture or Blancard's pills. Digitalis is often useful In many cases, cod oil is of value, and may be continued for months. We make choice, as required, of emulsion with pepsin and quinine, emulsion with phosphates, or plain oil.

Some degree of anorexia is always present, yet it may not prevent the regular meal, and need never occasion anxiety, for probably it will soon give place to a well-marked reverse condition, which may be encouraged to fullest feeding short of digestive disaster. The appetite often becomes enormous, and sometimes restraint and digestive aid are demanded. If it be slow in returning, rousing measures will suggest themselves. In such cases it has seemed a good plan to stir up the alvine system, once or twice a week for a time, with a mild cathartic at bedtime, or a full morning dose of hunyadi.

One result of the opiate-quitting and the régime noted is often a greatly improved nutrition, as shown by a notable increase in weight. One physician, not long since dismissed, gained a pound a day, and another convalescent has lately been adding to his avoirdupois at the rate of twelve pounds a fortnight.

Regarding the insomnia, Levinstein says: " Sleeplessness, which is generally protracted up into the fourth week, is very distressing." For reasons before given, his assertion is not surprising. Our record differs. Wakefulness is an invariable sequel, and requires soporifics for a time, but is not so prolonged and does not resist treatment. We have known a patient able to dispense with hypnotics in five days, others in eight, and nearly all within a fortnight. Sometimes, they are longer required. Two patients, both physicians, during the last year, did not regain natural sleep for three or four weeks, but this is quite exceptional.

This insomnia is of two kinds. Most patients, after the acute stage has been passed, soon secure sleep on retiring, but waken early —two or three o'clock,—and fail to get more. Others remain awake nearly all night before slumber comes, and these are the ones who usually require soporifics the longer.

For the relief of this, cannabis indica, or chloral with bromide, in full doses, serves our purpose. If, as rarely happens, the wakeful state is so pronounced or prolonged, despite treatment, as to distress the patient, we never hesitate to give a full opiate—*sub rosa*—and always with good result. In all cases, drugs should be dropped soon as possible, and sleep secured by a fatiguing walk, or other exercise, an electric séance, a Turkish or half hour's warm bath with cold douche or shower, a light meal or a glass or two of hot milk,—one or more of these before retiring.

Patients whose slumbers end early often note a peculiar depression on waking, and when such is the case, a lunch, milk, coffee, coca, or Murdoch's liquid food, should be at their command.

It may be well, in passing, to refer to certain minor sequelæ and their treatment. Occasionally a patient complains of dyspnœa, or palpitation. We have never noted them but twice—both ladies. A stimulant—coca with capsicum, or Hoffman's anodyne with aromat. spts. ammonia—will promptly control.

Some patients are, at times, annoyed by aching pains in the gastrocnemii, that may recur during several days. Fld. ext. gelseminum, in full doses, strong galvanic or faradic currents, massage, local hot baths, and topical use of chloroform or ether will relieve.

Others mention a peculiar burning in the

soles of the feet, which mustardized pediluvia and full doses of quinine usually control.

Sometimes a dry, hacking, paroxysmal cough, more marked at night, may discomfort a patient for a time. It can be relieved by nitrate of silver spray, ten to twenty grs. to the ounce ; a bromide of sodium gargle, sixty grs. to the ounce ; or a small blister to the sternum.

Returning sexual activity, as shown by nocturnal emissions and erections, as a rule, requires no attention. We once noted, however, a case where the awakened virile vigor was so marked that repressive measures were demanded.

The periodical function of females, which, usually, is irregular or suspended, has, so far as we have observed, required no special after-treatment.

Along with what has been suggested, should be such other general hygienic measures as will add to the good secured. Patients *must* be given attractive surroundings, cheerful society, diverting occupation and amusement, and freedom from care or worry of body and mind ; in fact any thing, every thing, that will aid in the effort to secure a return to pristine health and vigor. That the management of these

cases *subsequent* to the need of *active* professional care is of great importance, enlarged experience increasingly convinces. Neurotic or
other disorders noted prior to addiction,
whether genetic or not, must be relieved or removed. So, too, with those that may first
appear after the opiate-disusing; and when
none of these are met, when there is merely a
lessened power of brain and brawn, ample time
—months or years, if need be—must be taken
in which to get thoroughly well, if the chance
of a relapse would be brought to a minimum.

It is not to be supposed that a system shat-
tered by opiate excess will regain its normal
status within a week or a month, or that a
premature return to mental or physical labor
will not imperil the prospect of permanent cure.
The importance of this must be insisted upon.
To medical men, who compose so largely the
better class of habitués, it is especially commended. Professional work must not be resumed too soon. The frequency of a narcotic
return is in reverse relation to the length of
the opiate abstention, and, as favoring this abstinence, prolonged rest, change of scene, foreign travel, sea voyages, all have much promise
of good.

The absence of reference to certain remedies which have been mentioned by some as especially useful in the treatment of this neurosis may be briefly noted.

Belladonna has been supposed to have a special value. We once used it to the extent of dry mouth and disturbed vision during the opiate withdrawal, but have quite abandoned it, for the simple reason that we found, on trial, patients did fully as well without it, and the freedom from its peculiar effect certainly added to their comfort. Whatever its antagonistic influence in acute opium-taking, we do not believe it possesses any such virtue in the chronic form.

Quinine in large doses, from the outset, or grs. two to four, increasing with the opiate reduction, has been thought to have special value. We have failed to note it, though as a tonic it is well adapted to all cases, and in some patients, twenty-gr. doses, as an anodyne or soporific, act well.

Strychnine is another valued tonic, especially in a very gradual opiate decrease, or at weekly or fortnightly reductions. It has no other claim.

Hydrocyanic acid dilute, aconite, and veratrum viride have been suggested. Why, we fail to understand.

Jamaica dogwood has been commended as an opiate substitute, and Morse lauds it extravagantly. He, however, is an enthusiast, and, as such, goes quite too far.

Regarding its use, he says : " Coca cures the opium habit. Jamaica dogwood does more than this, it is prophylactic of this disorder. By its use the baneful habit is forbidden the system." This, we think, is a most mistaken opinion.

And, again : " As an hypnotic, opium is not of greater worth," and, "as an anodyne, opium is its only peer." Our experience is entirely contrary to any such assertions. We have made frequent trial of it ; the results were uneven. In a few cases—the minority,—as an anodyne it seemed efficient ; as an hypnotic it always failed. Morse puts the dose at "fld. ext.: dose min. v.-xv." Our ill result, certainly, was not due to the limited quantity, for we usually gave it in *two-drachm* doses. More recent trials have proved utter failures. One, as an anodyne in neuralgia, four one-drachm doses, half-hour interval, no relief whatever. Another, as a soporific ; six one-drachm doses, same interval, no sleep. It is a nauseous drug, and the aversion to continuing it may sometimes account for its failure. Our patients, too, may be peculiar, but, be that as it may, we have little faith in its value, and now seldom employ it.

Avena sativa has been largely lauded. We have given it again and again, in doses large and small, in water hot and cold, at intervals short and long, and always found it *worthless —absolutely good for nothing.* Bottle after bottle has been left with us by those who made trial of it in vain, and their experience accords with many who have written us, some of whom have taken it in *ounce* doses several times daily, and used *pounds* of it in the trial, without good ! ! ! Let no one be beguiled into a belief that oats fills the "long-felt want." A coming paper will, we think, quite disprove its vaunted virtue.

Hyoscyamia is a powerful drug, and in some cases may be of service. We once used it, but the need for it now seldom arises. Its employment should be limited to patients in good general condition, in whom the opiate-disusing is attended with unusual insomnia and motor activity, In such instances its good effect is sometimes surprising, bringing quiet and sleep with a promptness and power almost startling. We use Merck's amorphous, dose $\frac{1}{12}$ to $\frac{1}{6}$ of a grain hypodermically. This, in these patients, may be deemed the usual dose. With some, however, this causes a mild delirium without sleep, and in such cases the dose must be increased. Regarding its safety, Dr. John C. Shaw, Superintendent of the King's County Insane Asylum, has assured us that it is largely given in that institution with as little fear of ill effects as would attend the use of morphia.

The new alkaloid of Indian hemp, tannate of cannabin, commended by German authority, proved an entire failure in our hands.

The latest claimant for professional favor as a soporific is paraldehyde. Dujardin-Beaumetz lauds it, and claims special value in these cases, Our experience does not warrant such statements. In full doses, 4 to 8 grammes—60 to 120 minims—it sometimes brings sleep ; unlike chloral, in the early nights of the opium abstinence it does not excite. In most cases both are inferior to Indian hemp. It is best given in one half to one ounce of syrup, flavored with peppermint, ginger, or vanilla, and then added to a wineglassful or two of ice-water, or in capsule.

Non-mention of alcoholic stimulants has perhaps been noted. We rarely use them. The reason is varied. They are seldom called for. Very exceptionally, champagne, milk punch, or ale may be indicated, but our rule is, *never to use any form unless imperatively demanded;* and the advice of Levinstein, that " those who have an intense craving for alcoholic beverages may be allowed to drink wine in unlimited quantities," is, we think, *positively pernicious.* As Bartholow says :. " When the nervous system is losing the loved morphia impression it will take kindly to alcohol "; and he adds : " I especially warn the practitioner against a procedure which the patient will be inclined to adopt—that is, to take sufficient alcohol to cause a distinct impression on the nervous system in place of the morphia. This must result disastrously, for when the alcohol influence expires there will occur such a condition of depression that more alcohol will be necessary."

With these opinions we are quite in accord. The fact must not be forgotten that some habitués have used alcohol with morphia; others have taken morphia after addiction to the former; and, in general, habituation to any stimulant or narcotic begets a liability to take to another in case the original one is abandoned. As a factor in relapse, alcohol-taking ranks next to a re-use of opium. The risk, then, is obvious, and let the physician beware lest, in the effort to aid his patient in escaping one peril, he but involves him in another yet greater.

Some details of treatment, apart from the strictly remedial, may be of interest. Our rule in making the opiate decrease is not to inform the patient as to its progress, nor the actual time when it is ended. Better tell him when days have elapsed since the last dose, and then the assurance that so long a time has gone by since his enemy was routed will, of itself, be an aid in finishing the good work. The incredulous surprise with which this knowledge is received by some patients who have made frequent but futile efforts to escape, is quite notable.

As regards the manner of taking, a radical change is made. If hypodermically, the syringe is at once discarded and a sufficient

amount of morphia or opium given by mouth.
In many cases resort to the morphia or opium
can be made at once. If so, it should be done.
If not, their use giving rise to nausea, vomiting,
or headache, as exceptionally they may, the
usual method can be resumed for two or three
days, and then the bromide influence having
been secured in part, the syringe may be put
aside, and the opiate used without unpleasant
effect.

A German writer some time ago asserted
that many patients taking more than four
grains—.25 to .30 gramme—hypodermically,
daily, will get along fairly well with the same
amount of morphia by the mouth. We have
not found this to be the case. On the other
hand, three times the subcutaneous supply as
advised by Bartholow is more than enough.
An increase of one half or double the amount
will usually suffice.

Patients may demur to the change, but it
should be insisted on, for experience has
proven many points in its favor. In the first
place, we believe there is, with some, a certain
fascination about the syringe, which, once
ended, marks an advance towards success in
treatment. Many patients come to think that

the injections are absolutely essential, and to convince them to the contrary, as the change in taking will, inspires a feeling of gladsome relief and larger confidence in a happy result.

Again the *staying* power, so to speak, of morphia or opium by mouth is much greater than by subcutaneous taking. Of this there is no question. Morphia, hypodermically, is more quickly followed by the peculiar effect of the drug, which, too, is more decided, but earlier subsides, a higher acme sooner reached, to decline more rapidly; whereas, by the mouth, or in the form of opium, the rousing effect is more slowly developed, but it is on an evener plane, and more persistent. Patients accustomed to four to eight injections daily, will do well on two or three doses by mouth. One medical gentleman, now under treatment, who had been taking six injections daily, is doing perfectly well on one dose of opium by the mouth, night and morning.

As a rule, too, the change in taking brings about a marked improvement in the patients' condition. We have known them, after using the new method a few days, to declare that they felt better than for years. In many ways—

notably increased appetite and improved alvine action—is the change for good.

Still more, those who quit the syringe, and take morphia or opium, usually cross the Rubicon of their opiate-disusing with withdrawal symptoms so largely lessened as to make this result alone ample reason for the course we commend.

During the decrease, patients are permitted, if desired, to continue their frequency of taking. As a rule, however, by reason of the greater sustaining power of morphia or opium by the mouth, it is not required.

The only restriction imposed is that a certain amount shall suffice for twenty-four hours' supply, and this is daily decreased, according to individual need, at such a rate as will least likely conflict with their comfort. Patients, moreover, are always instructed that if the amount allowed does not suffice, they are to apply for and will be given more. Such being the case, no proper motive exists for secret taking, and if, despite this liberal proviso, it is indulged in, professional relations are suspended.

This being our plan, it will be inferred, and rightly, that we do not subject patients to such surveillance as compels their taking a bath, during which search is made for contraband morphia. Nor do we have an attendant "dogging" their steps during the decreasing régime. No person with proper self-respect would submit to such treatment without resenting it ; and it is not likely to strengthen the confidence that should always exist between patient and physician, and which, with us, is asked for and given. Very seldom is it violated. Patients come to us for relief ; they are willing to aid in the effort to secure it—those who are not we decline to accept—and the result is—success.

It is sometimes asserted that all opium habitués are liars, and that, on presenting themselves for treatment, they are always equipped with a syringe and a supply. Such a sweeping assertion we do not believe—*we know* it is *not true.* Why, then, should we humiliate them after such a fashion, degrade them by imposing such detective surroundings? Others may ; we will not, and as yet we have no reason to doubt the wisdom of our course.

Clandestine taking, either before or after withdrawal, can always be detected. The absence of certain invariable sequelæ of an honest quitting is positive proof of deception ; while the presence of morphia in the urine after the time when it should disappear, along with other symptoms, furnish added evidence beyond dispute.

It will again be inferred, and also aright, that we do not practise any such plan as Levinstein advises when he says: " As soon as the patient has consented to give up his personal liberty and the treatment is about to commence, he is to be shown into the room set apart for him for the period of eight to fourteen days, all opportunities for attempting suicide having been removed from them. Doors and windows must not move on hinges, but on pivots, must have neither handles nor bolts nor keys, being so constructed that the patients can neither open nor shut them. Hooks for looking-glasses, for clothes and curtains, must be removed. The bedroom, for the sake of control, is to have only the most necessary furniture ; a bed, devoid of protruding bedposts, a couch, an open wash-stand, a table furnished with alcoholic stimulants, champagne, port wine, brandy, ice in small pieces, and a tea urn with the necessary implements. In the room, which is to serve as a residence for the medical attendant for the first three days, the following drugs are to be kept under lock and key : a solution of morphia of two per cent., chloroform, ether, ammonia, liq. ammon. anis, mustard, an ice-bag, and an electric induction apparatus. A bathroom may adjoin these two apartments. During the first four or five days of the abstinence, the patient must be constantly watched by two female nurses."

Now what means this rigorous régime? First, that the lack of efficient medical measures makes essential physical force. Second, that the method employed entails such distress of mind and body as to risk a suicidal ending ; and that a great calamity always impends— collapse that threatens life, and demands that the doctor be closely at hand to avert the dreaded danger !

In strong contrast with what has been quoted, during our opiate withdrawal patients are not only permitted but encouraged to go out and about, attend entertainments, and engage in social domestic pleasures ; and this is continued throughout treatment, save a transient suspension following the first twenty-four hours of opium abstinence. After the first day of opium-disusing, patients are, for a time, under careful attention, and, if required, an attendant is with them, but the need for services of this sort is, usually, quite limited, and in some instances entirely dispensed with. Again and again have patients presented, who fully expected the rigorous régime imposed by Levinstein, but who were happily surprised to find it was not demanded, and who were fully convinced, before their treatment ended, that it was not at all essential.

As between this method and the barbarous plan of those who counsel and compel heroic withdrawal, "comparison is odious."

In this day of advanced therapeutics, the writer holds radical opinions as to the *utter in-excusability*, the *positive malpractice* of subjecting patients of this class to that torture of mind and body the German method entails. It is wrong, grievously wrong ; more, it is *cruel* to demand that they shall run the gauntlet of such suffering.

In various papers we have expressed our views on this important part of the subject, and enlarged experience tends only to confirm them. More and more pronounced is our belief " that no physician is warranted, save under circumstances peculiar and beyond control, in subjecting his patient to the torturing ordeal of abrupt withdrawal. We are well aware that it has the sanction of men otherwise eminent in the profession, but we venture to suggest, with no lack of respect to these gentlemen, that theory is one thing, practice another, and we are quite certain, were *they* compelled to undergo the trial, there would be a rapid and radical change of opinion. We regard it as cruel, barbarous, *utterly unworthy the healing art.'*

" We care not who advocates it, but speak feelingly, emphatically, and advisedly on this point, for the simple reason that our experience, again and again repeated, proves beyond all dispute that the opium habitué can be brought out of his bondage without any such crucial suffering as this method of treatment entails."

Bartholow says : " Having had one experience of this kind, I shall not be again induced to repeat it, if for no other, for strictly humanitarian reasons, since the mental and physical sufferings are truly horrible."

For proof of this and more in detail, the reader is referred to papers by the writer : "Clinical Notes on Opium Addiction," *Cincinnati Lancet and Clinic*, March 3, 1883 ; " Neurotic Pyrexia with Special Reference to Opium Addiction," *New England Medical*

Monthly, June, 1883; "The Treatment of Opium Addiction," *St. Louis Courier of Medicine*, June, 1883; and "A Personal Narrative of Opium Addiction," *New York Med. Gazette*, July 7, 1883.

More, many unaware that a more humane method is at command, and dreading the ordeal of abrupt disusing, refuse to accept it, and, continuing their narcotic, bind all the more closely "the web that holds them fast as fate." During the past year, a medical gentleman nine years addicted to morphia came under our care. Six years ago he first consulted us. During this time he had read Levinstein's book, and the dread of such suffering as that author's patients underwent was, he avowed, the reason for his delay in making an effort to quit the morphia. Finally, summoning sufficient courage—though not without much apprehension—the trial was made, and with the most gratifying success, for, greatly to his surprise, and pleasure, he made a notably good recovery with so little nervous disturbance that not a single bath was called for, and with such freedom from pain that not once was an anodyne demanded, and was dismissed on the twenty-sixth day of his treatment. Commenting on his case, he declared the manner of his recovery seemed "almost miraculous," and asserted that, had he ever thought so much could be accomplished at so little cost of time and discomfort, his effort, years earlier, would have been made; and in a recent letter he wrote : " My own swift and easy passage of that ' one more river to cross,' is an ever-recurring source of wonder and astonishment to me, and not a day passes, not a morning comes, without a keen sense of exultation at my escape from the old slavery, a blessed freedom from the old self-accusing conscience, and a return of the old instinctive habit of looking every man straight in the eyes !   I think I shall never entirely get rid of a certain shadow of the past ; nearly nine years of mental distress, which I thought wellnigh hopeless, must leave a deep and ugly scar at my time of life, but thank God that I have only the scar to trouble my memory, and not the festering, corroding, ever-present ulcer which made me unspeakably wretched, and kept me in continual fear of discovery."

Before closing, let it be noted that this, beyond question, is a vincible disease, and re-assert—*vide* " Opium Addiction among Medical Men,"—that " repeated experience warrants the assertion that every case of opium addiction free from organic disease, and in which there is an earnest desire to recover—be the extent and duration what it may—admits of prompt and positive relief."